0 03 03 0282308 0

W9-DHG-974

SELF-DEFENSE FOR WOMEN

by
Willy Cahill

I would like to dedicate this book to my family who believed in me all these years: my son Curtis and his wife Lisa; my grandchildren Jonathan, Michelle, Nicholas and Noelle; my daughter Carin and her husband Ken; and especially my wife Ellie, my biggest critic and also my biggest supporter.

©Ohara Publications, Incorporated 1978
All rights reserved
Printed in the United States of America
Library of Congress Catalog Number: 96-072480
ISBN # 0-89750-061-X

Fourth printing 2002

OHARA 🔲 PUBLICATIONS, INCORPORATED
SANTA CLARITA, CALIFORNIA

Champions

Champions are not born, they possess the desire to excel.
To be successful in anything, it takes quality hard work,
self-discipline and careful planning.

ACKNOWLEDGEMENTS

I would like to thank Mr. John Quinn, my assistant instructor, for the time and extra help he gave me in putting this book together. Also Laurie McRae for working with John and me prior to the final photo session we had in Burbank.

Thanks also to David Jennings, Mike Kessler, Ingrid Nugent, Jimmy Williams, Joe Wald, Mark Lavalle, Sandy and Angelo Sacconaghi, Kelly and Deinie Derbin and Carin Cahill for taking time out to put this book together. These are students of mine, some working on self-defense for the first time.

These people who are involved with the book had only one hour of practice prior to the photo session. The oldest was my mother-in-law, Dorothy Caton, who is 65 years old. Also George and Kathy Barron, Phil and Darlene Sullivan, Jim Gallagher, Mike Abelar, Bill Hjerpe, Lisa Goldman, Virginia Goodrich, Rene Kessler, Debbie Tracey, Carolyn Wald and Rick Benedet.

I also want to thank Mr. and Mrs. Don Nugent for the use of their home and car for some of the attack and escape scenes for this book.

Special thanks to Mr. Don Frate and Frank Haggarty for the use of Tanforan Shopping Center in San Bruno, California, where most of the photos were taken. Also the Fox Security Guards for their help in keeping control of the spectators while the photos were taken in that shopping center.

ABOUT THE AUTHOR

Willy Cahill began his martial arts education under his father, Professor John Cahill Sr., who founded Cahill's Judo Academy in Daly City, California, in 1948. Professor Cahill was one of the most highly respected instructors ever to come out of Professor Harry S. Ozaki's Kodenkan System of Jujitsu in Hawaii. In 1962, Professor Cahill passed away at a very young 50 years of age. In 1963, Willy built the new dojo in San Bruno, California, in his father's honor. At this club, Cahill set new standards and goals for himself and his students. In 1970, students from this dojo won the first of nine consecutive California State Judo Championships and the first of five consecutive United States Judo Association National Championships.

From 1963 to 1996, Cahill has produced over 800 National and International medal winners. His Elite Athletes have represented the United States at numerous international events. While Cahill was judo coach at both San Francisco State and Stanford University, the women's judo team at San Francisco State won the Collegiate National Championships.

In addition to the consecutive State and National Team Championships, several of Cahill's students have achieved individual success. This began in 1967 when George Golda won a bronze medal at the U.S. Junior National Championships in Miami. In 1968, Golda won a silver medal in Long Beach, and in 1969 he won a gold medal in Denver. He thus became the first student from Cahill's Judo Academy to win a National Championship. Two years later, in 1971, Cahill's baby-sitter Devi Nelson became his first senior National Champion, winning a gold medal in Los Angeles. In 1975, Cahill was inducted into the Black Belt Hall of Fame as Judo Instructor of the Year. In 1976, Mike Kessler won a bronze medal at the Junior World Championships in Madrid,

Spain. The women's World Judo Championships were held for the first time in 1980. Monica Emmerson represented the United States at these championships, which were held in New York. In 1983, Brett Barron won the gold medal at the Pan American Games in Caracas, Venezuela. One year later, Brett represented the United States at the Olympic Games in Los Angeles. John Matsuoka won a bronze medal at the World University Games in Belgium in 1990.

But one of the brightest achievements in Willy's career was seeing his student, Corinne Shigemoto, named to the coaching staff of the 1992 women's U.S. Olympic judo team, then named head coach of the 1996 women's U.S. Olympic judo team. The achievement was symbolic of handing over the reigns to the next generation, for after serving as assistant coach for the 1984 and 1988 men's U.S. Olympic judo teams, Willy declined the position of head coach for the 1992 men's U.S. Olympic judo team.

Willy coached his first International team in 1976 when he traveled with the U.S. team to Mexico City for the Junior Pan American Championships. He eventually coached the U.S. Team at the 1983 and 1987 Pan American Games, the 1983 and 1985 Pacific Rim Championships, and the 1986 and 1990 Goodwill Games. He also coached the World Championship teams in 1981, '85, '87, '89 and '91. He has taken U.S. judo teams to Europe and the former Eastern Block countries, including East Germany, Hungary, Poland, Czechoslovakia, Yugoslavia and the Soviet Union. And he has taken U.S. judo teams to Japan, Korea and Hong Kong several times.

In 1996, Cahill produced a set of three videotapes titled "Willy Cahill's Judo Training Series." Several of Willy's students demonstrated the techniques in the videos, which provide an overview of judo from beginning basics to advanced moves.

Cahill also in 1996 opened The World of Martial Supplies, a company specializing in martial arts supplies, weapons, uniforms, exercise and training equipment, videos, and nutritional and herbal products. The nutritional products are aimed at helping the athlete achieve his optimum level in health as well as performance; and improving his genral health, well-being and energy level. Many of America's professional and Olympic athletes are using them.

PUBLISHER'S PREFACE

If you are a female and you live in or around a major city, you may have experienced some anxious moments in which you worried about becoming the victim of violence.

No matter how often or eloquently influential figures may decry the rising tide of street violence, they cannot legislate a more humane attitude; perpetrators of violence are the wrong people to look to for mercy. Although there are no heartening signs that the numbers of violent incidents are diminishing, we hope this book will deliver a message of hope.

Every attack situation is different, but a growing consensus of psychiatrists, police and women seems to indicate that the odds of survival are with the woman who chooses to fight back. Of course, there are limitations to this idea. If you weigh 100 pounds, for example, you probably shouldn't fight back with your 200-pound attacker. So we recommend that you disrupt the attack as fiercely and thoroughly as possible, then make yourself scarce. This book offers you practical advice and presents it in a way which we hope will encourage you to believe in the idea of limited resistance.

If you are attacked you will either panic or fight back, but your enemies are both visible and invisible. Not only must you fight the one who accosts you, you must also battle the invisible enemies of hopelessness and helplessness. Finding a victim who will go limp with helpless terror is a mugger's perverse dream. Although we can't say that you, whatever your size, will be able to break every bone in your attacker's body when you've finished this book, we can provide descriptions of a few helpful kicks and punches. We hope you will never have to use them in a life-or-death situation. However, this book may give you more peace of mind and help you take comfort in the fact that you are not clay in the hands of every shifty-looking character you pass on the street. And remember, men are just as subject to pain as women—perhaps more so.

To become an expert in any form of self-defense requires several hundred hours of practice. If you know little or nothing about how to protect yourself, maybe this book will be an inspiration. Attacks can be avoided, forestalled and resisted. Practice some of the techniques demonstrated in this book, and you may begin to feel less afraid and more courageous. There is a clearheadedness that accompanies self-confidence. And in stressful situations, that clearheadedness is a valuable weapon.

Above all, keep in mind that all violent people definitely bleed and bruise.

Author Willy Cahill, a family man with a black belt in both judo and jujitsu, says it very plainly: "I believe a little knowledge is better than none at all. Train yourself in some basics."

INTRODUCTION

The popularity of martial arts training in the United States today is due to motion pictures, television, demonstrations and the growing public awareness that for those who get and stay with it, martial arts training is very effective. Practitioners of the arts and sports of karate, kung fu, judo, jujitsu, aikido, hapkido, tae kwon do and other forms and styles have been, by and large, excellent salesmen.

It is impossible to say which of the arts is best. Ideally, one chooses whatever will be efficient in the face of danger, and increasingly in the Americanization of the essentially Asian martial arts, this has been so. Using whatever works seems to be the trend.

But remember, what you study as self-defense must work for you. Only you can make a thing happen by the amount of time and energy you devote to training. Having a positive attitude, one that reflects a curiosity and desire to know, will also be of assistance in your desire to excel.

First, you must realize that this book is not intended to make you an expert. Its purpose is to instill confidence and give you an adequate basic skill that will prepare you for meeting with unavoidable situations.

I wrote this book to illuminate situations that do arise, to help you meet ugly circumstances and escape impending danger or death. Yet it would be impossible to write a complete self-defense book because of the almost infinite number of situations in which a woman may find herself vulnerable. Learn enough to be able to adapt, to respond to any situation instinctively.

You can help yourself by making a survey based on attacks of which you've learned. Answer these questions about them. When did it happen? Where? Was it day or night? Did the victim try to defend herself? If not, why not? If so, what kind of techniques did she use? How effective were her responses? How skilled was she at being able to protect herself?

In spite of all we read, see and hear about these violent crimes, not enough people are studying a means of self-defense. I am convinced that it should be a part of the curriculum in physical education in every school and in all adult classes. In addition to learning how to save your life or the lives of people around you, practicing self-defense tones muscles and builds robust health.

I believe that a little knowledge is better than none at all. Train yourself in some basics, and teach yourself to respond and react instantly. Time must be made to work for you. Freezing up or panicking works against you. The instant you succumb to terror or paralysis, you become clay in the attacker's hands. Surprise your enemy. Speed and surprise work for you and against him. Screaming may scare him, may bring help, but it may also galvanize him into action. Handle each situation as the occasion warrants. To do that, you must be prepared.

To overcome the paralysis that usually follows fear, you must jump into action. Show your attacker you know what you're doing. If he thinks you're going to kick the hell out of him, he may abandon the scheme immediately. Attackers feel their victims are vulnerable, powerless and without defensive resources. They put their trust in the idea that they can overpower their victims with ease. Concerning the untrained, this is usually all too true. Therefore, you must train and prepare yourself.

Analyze yourself and see if you are a potential victim because of your daily routine. Do you dress so you can run, have freedom of movement? Can you land a telling kick or punch? Do you hitch rides? Do you walk dimly lit streets alone? Do you carry cumbersome handbags? Do you know how to call an emergency telephone operator? Do you lock yourself in your car? Do you open the window only a crack if someone has to talk to you? Do you walk in groups? Do you look around and observe the people behind you?

It takes two people to make for street tragedy. What kind of victim would you be if you were attacked? Would you be helpless or prepared to protect yourself? If you choose to protect yourself, then you must prepare physically and mentally. You must practice your self-defense skills until they become second nature. Then you will have the confidence needed to protect yourself.

That's what this book is all about. That is what self-defense courses are all about. Recruit a friend and practice.

When consulted by a few girls in a publishing firm office about the most effective defense against a sudden mugging attack, Bruce Lee, as was his manner, came to the point of his advice quickly. "Kick 'em in the knee and run like hell," he advised.

It's sound advice. It promises to disable the attacker as quickly as possible, and as a fiercely aggressive approach, it reminds the listener that the whole idea of self-defense is to end a fight before it begins. It may well be the soundest advice ever offered on this difficult subject.

Although he tossed off the remark and made it sound rather easy, there is a bit more to landing a proper kick on the knee and running than first appears. You must know where to kick, how to kick, how much force it takes to disable a person and give you a good chance of getting away. But most important, your reaction must be spontaneous. And how do you respond instantly if pushed, grabbed or choked? You need to find out, because usually the attack, like the defense, is all over in a matter of seconds.

Not long ago, a young woman walked into my studio and told me that one night she had been attacked. Fortunately, she was able to escape. Why? Because she reacted instantly.

The scene was Ohio in late winter. It had been snowing earlier, but that night the weather had cleared, and the lady in question had decided to go to a movie with a girl friend. While she was walking across an open lot, a man came out of the dark and grabbed her. She kicked him in the knee, and with all her strength pushed him to the ground and ran. She remembered that it was hard to run in high-heeled shoes. So she kicked them off and ran. Her biggest disappointment, as she expressed it to me later, was that she had just bought the shoes a few days earlier—before being asked to sacrifice them.

Later that night, having reported the incident to the police, she found herself accused of having instigated the incident. The police refused to seek charges against the man who attempted the attack. A couple of days later, when she walked into a grocery store, she saw her assailant. He was one of the checkers at a cash register. She left the store, warned her friends and never heard anything more of the incident. Because of the police department's attitude, she felt she needed self-confidence that comes from mastering self-defense.

First, we analyzed the situation and her reaction to the attack. Our goal in doing this was to find out how she could improve on her response should she ever again find herself in a similar situation. When she kicked him and pushed him down, she had a good opportunity to kick him again and make sure he wouldn't recover quickly. Next, when she removed her shoes, she didn't realize that she was discarding an excellent pair of weapons—the high heels make wonderfully effective clubs when held in the hands. Fortunately, she was the winner on this occasion.

We also discussed physical fitness, diet and exercise. She conceded that when she felt good physically she was more alert. She would probably live longer that way, even without her course in self-defense.

Then I outlined the course for her. Here it is. In each lesson, she learns some new way to use her legs, hands, arms, feet and body to defend herself from attack. In each lesson, she learns three or four options in striking, kicking, throwing and in responding to simulated attacks. These strengthen her ability to defend herself. The basic moves give her a versatility in choosing options that would fit any occasion.

There is no right or wrong way to defend yourself. Make it work; to do the job is the important thing.

Remember these rules.

1) When you kick, kick with power.

2) When you strike, strike with speed.

3) When you run, run with the wind rather than against it.

Willy Cahill
San Bruno, California
July 1978

CONTENTS:

CHAPTER I

KICK 'EM WHERE IT WILL HURT

In this chapter we will concentrate on the front kick, the back kick, the side kick and the sidestep kick. All of these kicks are easy to learn if you follow the step-by-step movements. But it is essential that you remember to practice the kicks and movements with good *balance, accuracy* and (later) *SPEED*.

In order to develop effective kicks, they must become second nature to you. Basic kicks are your automatic response to an attack. A strong, fast and effective kick, accurately placed, is one of your best lines of defense.

It is much easier for him to get away from a punch if you are standing at a safe distance from your attacker. But a well-placed kick will be a lot tougher for the attacker to evade.

This chapter concentrates on the practical application of each kick. Simulated attacks are demonstrated. You should learn each kick for use in an actual attack situation. Get a partner to practice with you. Work out the form first. Mark it. Learn it. Then develop accuracy, power and speed. If you do that in the order set forth—first, form; second, accuracy; third, power, and fourth, speed—you will have a satisfactory arsenal of self-defense against attack. Remember, seconds count. In most cases, it's all over in less than 10 seconds.

FRONT KICK

If it appears that you are in for a fight, you will need to launch a series of front kicks to show your attacker you mean business and intend to defend yourself. For this you should take a solid stance that will add strength, speed and accuracy to your counterattacks.

CLOSE-UP

Note how she brings her right leg up, bending at the knee before she executes the front kick. Now she can easily kick powerfully without losing her balance.

INDIVIDUAL

(1) The basic stance has the front foot forward, knee bent slightly, the back leg comfortably poised and arms ready to protect against a punch or to block a kick. (2) From this position, bring the back leg forward, cocking at the

DEMONSTRATION

(1) The attacker grabs the victim by both hands and tries to pull her towards him. (2) She tries to pull away and free her hands from his strong grip. (3) Note how she has crouched into a good defensive stance to launch a powerful

knee: the weight has shifted to your front foot (3). Now you quickly execute an accurate, powerful and fast kick to the attacker.

and accurate front kick. (4) She cocks the leg and launches the kick. The groin and stomach are obvious targets, but the shin, knee and chest are also suitable.

1

2

3

ACTION
IN THE
STREET

The victims walk down the street on their way to school. (2) Suddenly the attacker jumps out of a car and (3) grabs the young girl and tries to drag her into the car. But (4) the victim has other ideas; as soon as the at-

4

tacker grabs her wrist and tries to pull her, he finds out that it is impossible. Quickly (5) she gets into a set position for a front kick and (6) kicks her attacker in the groin.

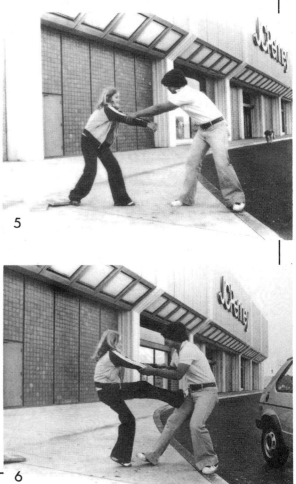

5

6

BACK KICK

The back kick requires a more complete commitment and takes a great deal more practice to perfect. It is best launched from an effective stance position.

CLOSE-UP

Note the position of the balance foot. It is pointing in the opposite direction for power and better balance.

INDIVIDUAL

(1&2) As you look back, lean slightly forward away from the attacker; then bring your left hand up to protect your midsection, while clenching into a fist to protect the upper body. Bend your left knee slightly, while bending your body forward as you (3) cock the right leg. Note that your hands and arms

DEMONSTRATION

(1) The victim is shown walking down the street when suddenly the attacker grabs her purse and attempts to pull it from her shoulder. (2) From this position she looks back at the attacker and starts to lean forward and away from him. (3) She then lets the purse slide to the crook of the elbow. (4)

ACTION IN THE STREET

(1) This time the potential victim is walking through the shopping center with her purse around her shoulder. (2) The attacker reaches out to grab her purse from the rear and attempts to pull the purse off her shoulder. (3) As he tugs, she lets it slide to the crook of her elbow; using the tension as leverage, she balances on her front foot, leans forward, then suddenly strikes his stomach.

protect you against kicks or possible strikes from your attacker. (4) Launch the kick accurately with power and speed. Practice this and other kicks until they are smooth and flow readily. Use a target such as a pillow.

Placing most of her weight on the front foot, she starts to bend her kicking leg. Now she balances on the front leg, brings her back leg up and kicks the attacker in the stomach.

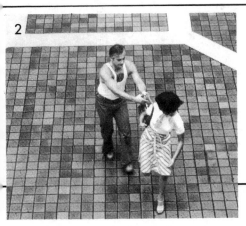

SIDE KICK

CLOSE-UP

When you apply the side step kick, your balance foot should be pointed slightly to the left to give you more leverage and better balance. This also makes the kick more effective.

INDIVIDUAL

(1) The basic stance for launching a side kick is to lean away from the assailant while blocking your face and body with your hands. Step towards the attacker by placing your left foot in back of your right while still protect-

DEMONSTRATION

(1) Assailant approaches and grabs the victim by the wrist and she immediately starts to pull away. (2) He attempts to pull her towards him, and she closes her fist to resist his pull and steps towards him by placing her left foot in back of her right foot. (3) Now she leans away from the attacker and brings her right leg up, kicking the attacker in the groin.

ing your body. (2) Bring your right foot up while bending at the knee. Keep your left foot pointing away from your kick for better balance, and (3) strike the attacker with your right foot to his abdomen or groin.

1

2

ACTION IN THE STREET

(1) The attacker watches as the victim walks by and then suddenly lunges at her, grabbing her wrist. (2) She brings her right leg up and kicks the

3

attacker in the groin, using a side kick, then (3) extending her kick by leaning into it, (4) forces the attacker to fall on his back.

4

SIDE STEP
KICK

INDIVIDUAL

(1) From a basic stance, take a step to your left front and (2) bring your right hand up to block a possible punch. (3) Balance on your left foot and (4) cock

DEMONSTRATION

(1) The victim is confronted by her attacker. (2) She dodges to one side to get away from his oncoming punch. From here she can easily block a punch (3) and push the attacker away from her. (4) While blocking, she starts to

the right leg for the kick. Extend the kicking leg forward, (5) and kick the attacker in the stomach.

bring up her kicking leg. Now she can kick the attacker's stomach. The same kick may be used as a secondary attack to the groin.

1

ACTION IN THE STREET

(1&2) In these photos we show the victim walking through the shopping center when suddenly an assailant lashes out with a right-hand punch. She steps out of the way of the oncom-

2

3

ing punch and quickly blocks it with her right arm. (3) Pushing the right hand away from her face, she delivers (4) a side step kick.

4

CHAPTER II

STRIKING

We will use the word strike instead of punch in this book, because a punch is often thought of as a straight-line blow like those delivered by a boxer. Defending yourself, however, you will be striking from all different directions and with a number of different techniques. Although a punch is ordinarily associated with the closed fist, most women simply do not have the power to knock a man unconscious. Then, too, even a professional boxer protects and tapes his hands and wrists before he steps into the ring.

The important thing for you to learn is how to use your hands without building them up to become lethal weapons. By learning to employ your hands and arms with speed and timing, and by delivering each blow to a vital zone on the aggressor's body, you can make your strikes very effective for self-defense purposes.

I will teach you three different strikes to be used at different times and under various circumstances, but you must learn to deliver them all with force, speed and power, to deliver them accurately to sensitive targets.

The overhead strike is delivered with a closed fist and a downward motion, as you would drive a nail with a hammer. Strike the top of the head, as though you were trying to pound your assailant into the ground. Most effective when an attacker is about to throw a punch or trying to reach out and grab you with one hand, the overhead strike can be used by blocking his reach with one arm and striking him with the other.

The openhand strike is delivered with an upward motion starting at the chin, as if you were trying to knock your assailant's head off his shoulders. In what we call an openhand strike, you bend your fingers down to the top of the palm. Hold your thumb tightly against your fingers as if you were pushing inward. Strike with the base of the palm. This strike is best used when the attacker pulls you toward him. Using his pull, you can strike with the open hand.

The forearm strike is just that, a strike with the forearm. With a closed fist pointing downward, you use your forearm, striking in an upward motion to the throat, chin or face. If the attacker steps backward and you should miss, you can pivot slightly and strike with your elbow.

OVERHEAD STRIKE

CLOSE-UP

Notice the striking hand is in a closed fist and the direction of the strike is downward. Using the hand as though you were striking with a hammer, employ the bottom of the hand as a weapon.

INDIVIDUAL

(1) From the basic stance, the forward foot points straight ahead with the knee slightly bent. The back leg is straight and points outward at a slight angle. The left hand is in a closed fist in front of the chest, fist pointing downward, the right hand closed in a fist held close to the hip. (2) Bring the

DEMONSTRATION

(1) Notice the victim is in a basic stance. (2) She blocks the straight punch being delivered by the attacker with her left arm and (3) starts to force his arm in a downward motion while bringing her right hand up for the strike. (4)

left hand up, blocking a straight punch. Raise it higher to push the striking hand away from you and (3) start the right hand in an upward motion for the strike. (4) Forcing his striking hand down and away from you, (5) hammer the attacker on the top of his head.

She applies a lot of pressure with her left hand on his striking arm and brings her other hand down on the top of the attacker's head, striking the top of his head with all possible force.

ACTION IN THE STREET

(1) The intended victim is looking over the railing in a shopping center when she notices a stranger looking at her in a crude way; he starts to approach her from the side. (2) As he puts his arm around her shoul-

3

der, she removes his arm with a left elbow strike to his ribs, (3) then comes down on his head with the overhead strike. (4) Now she can easily bring up a knee to his groin.

4

OPENHAND STRIKE

CLOSE-UP

Notice the striking hand. The fingers are curled down to the palm of the hand and the thumb is held close to the side and pushing in towards the palm. The strike will be delivered in an upward motion, striking the attacker on the chin.

1

INDIVIDUAL

(1) From the basic stance, she brings her left arm (2) up to block a punch. As she forces the attacker's strike to the side, (3) she raises her right arm. By

DEMONSTRATION

(1) The victim again assumes a basic stance. The attacker strikes the victim, (2) but the punch is blocked with the left forearm. (3) Now the victim brings her right hand up while pushing the attacker's hand away with her left fore-

now, she has completely forced the attacker's hand away, (4) and delivers her right hand up in an openhand upward strike to the attacker's chin.

arm. (4) She throws her right hand up to the attacker's chin, forcing his head to fall backward, striking while in an upward motion. (5) From here she can easily follow through with an elbow to the face or a knee to the groin.

ACTION IN THE STREET

(1) The victim is coming out of the store when she is approached by a stranger. (2) He grabs her by the wrist and attempts to pull her towards him. (3&4) Quickly she turns to face her attacker and strikes him with an openhand strike to the chin, (5) forcing the attacker to fall back.

1

3

2

4

5

FOREARM STRIKE

CLOSE-UP

In the forearm strike, you bring your right forearm in front of your chest then strike the victim with your forearm. Notice the closed fist, with the fist pointing downward and the left hand held close to the side.

INDIVIDUAL

(1) Again from the basic stance, she brings her left hand (2) up to block a punch. (3) Now the right hand comes up, using the forearm strike. She raises

DEMONSTRATION

(1) The victim is approached by a stranger, and she immediately gets into a defensive stance. The attacker (2) attempts to grab the victim around the waist and starts (3) to pull the victim towards him. She leans towards the

her left arm up against her side, (4) then follows through with the forearm.

attacker by bending her forward knee slightly (4) and starts to bring her right arm up to her side in an upward motion. (5) Now she strikes the attacker in the face with her right forearm.

ACTION IN THE STREET

(1) The victim is walking through the shopping center when she is approached by an attacker who attempts to punch her in the face. Quickly she blocks the punch with her left arm, (2) strikes her attacker with a forearm across the

face, (3&4) brings her right knee up to his groin. Forcing the attacker's head back, she brings her knee still higher (5). She can also hit the attacker with an elbow strike across the face or throat.

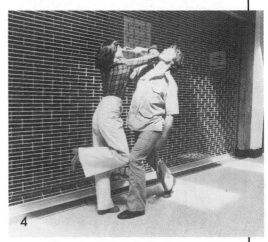

CHAPTER III

BREAKING THE ATTACK TO ESCAPE

In this chapter I have compiled a number of practical application situations. You could be faced with any one of them almost anywhere, at any time. With a little practice, however, you will be able to *react instantly* with an *effective response.*

Foremost in your mind should be stopping the attacker, immobilizing the thug and gaining a chance to escape and seek help —if that's the best course of action. It is vital that you respond with *speed, accuracy, good balance and a clear mind. Block, strike, immobilize and escape:* these are four quick and effective foundations on which to base your instinctive self-defense plan.

There are many situations in which you could be attacked. It would have been impossible to cover them all in this book, but all of the basic movements and counterattacks covered here can be effectively applied whatever the circumstances. By now you should have an effective arsenal of self-defense. Use it. Keep it simple. Practice it. Don't get rusty. Stay in shape.

Remember this, your greatest enemy is fear. Fear can cause you to lose control of yourself, paralyze you and easily bring about your defeat. That's why you must make your response one of automatic reflex—that takes daily practice.

1

FRONT GRAB
ARMS FREE

(1) The victim is approached from the front by an attacker who (2) reaches out to grab her around the waist. (3) She brings up both arms, rapping the assailant sharply

2

3

on both ears, then (4) reaches up to grab his hair while lifting her right knee, (5) tearing at his hair and delivering a knee kick simultaneously.

4

5

FRONT GRAB, ARMS LOCKED

(1) The assailant approaches his victim from the front and (2) grabs her around the waist, locking her arms to her side. Now (3) she brings

her right leg up along his left shin, bringing her heel (4) down sharply on the top of his foot. (5) Following up, she knees him sharply to the groin.

REAR GRAB, ARMS LOCKED

(1) Encircling her arms, the attacker grabs his victim about the waist. (2) She twists sharply, loosening his grip and kicking him in the shin. As he reapplies his grip, (3) she steps to one side, doubles up a fist, and (4) strikes him in the groin. (5) Now she kicks again, this time to the kneecap.

1

3

2

4

5

REAR GRAB, ARMS FREE

(1) The attacker grabs his victim around the waist. Quickly, before he can secure a strong grip, she stoops (2) and leaning backward into her assailant, (3) she snatches an ankle, causing him (4) to topple backwards, (5) from which position she delivers a back kick to his groin.

LYING ON HER SIDE

(1) The victim is reading a magazine when an aggressive man rushes up to her. (2) Quickly she moves her right foot around to encircle her attacker's right heel while drawing her left leg back and bending at the knee. Positioning her right foot against the inside of the attacker's kneecap (3) and pulling with the other foot, which is wrapped around his ankle—see close-up (4), she is able to (5) force him to the ground.

LYING ON HER BACK

(1) The victim is lying on her back in the sun when she is approached by an attacker. (2) She sits partly up, supporting her weight on her forearms, pulls back with her right leg, bending at the knee, and (3) delivers a kick as shown in different view, (4&5) causing the attacker to roll backwards in his pain.

BREAKING
THE ATTACK

SIDE HAIR PULL

(1) While waiting for a friend, a victim is approached abruptly from the side. (2) An attacker reaches out to grab her by the hair, but she reaches up with her left arm to hold his wrist in position. Then (3) she draws her right arm

FRONT HAIR PULL

(1) The victim is walking through a shopping center hoping to walk past a suspicious-looking character, but (2) he reaches out to pull her hair and yank her toward him. She grabs his wrist to make sure he cannot easily retreat, (3)

back and, (4) twisting and turning his forearm, delivers a hammer strike to the back of his elbow, forcing him to the ground, (5) where she follows with a kick to the back.

lifts her right leg, bending it at the knee, and (4) delivers a front kick to his groin.

DOOR DEFENSE

(1) Be on guard when you answer the door, particularly if you don't know the person there. As you talk with a stranger, keep your left foot positioned to act as a door jamb. (2) As the aggressor tries to bull his way in, step slightly off to one side, brace yourself and (3) deliver a hard, snapping front kick to his groin.

DOOR BLOCK AND ARM BAR

(1) Again, step beside the door to use your foot as a jamb. (2) This time, as he reaches in to try to grab you, hang on to the doorknob tightly, and taking hold on the backside of his wrist, and making use of your leg, foot, hip and

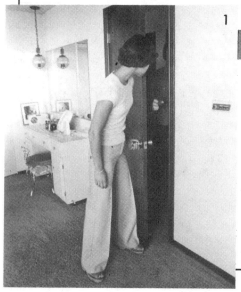

the doorknob, (3) slam or push hard against the door until (4) you are in a position to break his arm.

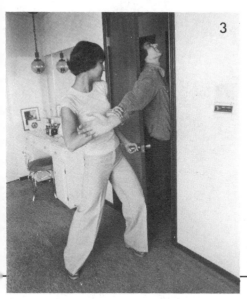

SITTING POSITION ARM AROUND SHOULDER

(1) The victim is sitting down when a man sitting beside her puts his arm around her shoulder. (2) Slowly she takes his hand and lifts it over her head. Retaining her grip on his wrist, she brings his arm in front of her, (3&4) and knocks him forward with a left forearm to the back of his elbow. (5) Hanging on to her wrist grip, she applies more pressure and forces him down face first.

1

3

2

4

5

SITTING POSITION HAND ON KNEE

(1) We see the victim sitting on a bench waiting for a bus when she is approached by the assailant, who (2) sits down beside her and tries to start a conversation. Ignored, (3) he puts a hand on her knee. She places her hand over his to hold it in place, then (4&5) pulling on his arm, twisting his wrist and retaining her grip, she strikes the back of his elbow with her left forearm, forcing him down on his face (6). (7) The assailant is rendered harmless.

SITTING IN A CAR

(1) A young lady is sitting in her car when (2) an attacker reaches in through an open window and grabs her around the throat. (3) She leans away from him, escapes his grip and traps his

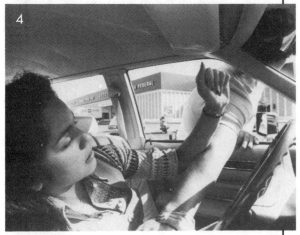

right arm, taking hold of it and guiding it toward the front of the car. By pulling his arm toward her (4), and striking him behind the elbow with her forearm (5), she can easily break his arm.

GETTING INTO A CAR

(1) While getting into her car, a woman is approached by a stranger who (2) opens the door wider in an effort to

climb in beside her, but (3) she falls back on the front seat and (4) lands a fierce kick to the assailant's groin.

4

PARKING LOT ATTACK SIDE KICK

(1) A woman walking to her car with a bag of groceries is being followed by a stranger who reaches out (2) and grabs her purse. She drops her bag and, allowing her purse to slide to the crook of her elbow, (3) balances on her left foot, bends her right leg at the knee and, (4) continuing to bend her knee and raise her leg (5&6) lands a side kick to her assailant's groin. A second kick (7&8) to the inside of his knee knocks him right to the ground.

PARKING LOT ATTACK BACK KICK

(1) The woman is about to put a bag of groceries in her trunk when an attacker approaches her from the rear. (2) He reaches out and puts his

3

hands on her shoulders, but (3&4) she balances herself with the help of the trunk, raises her right leg and back kicks her attacker to the groin.

4

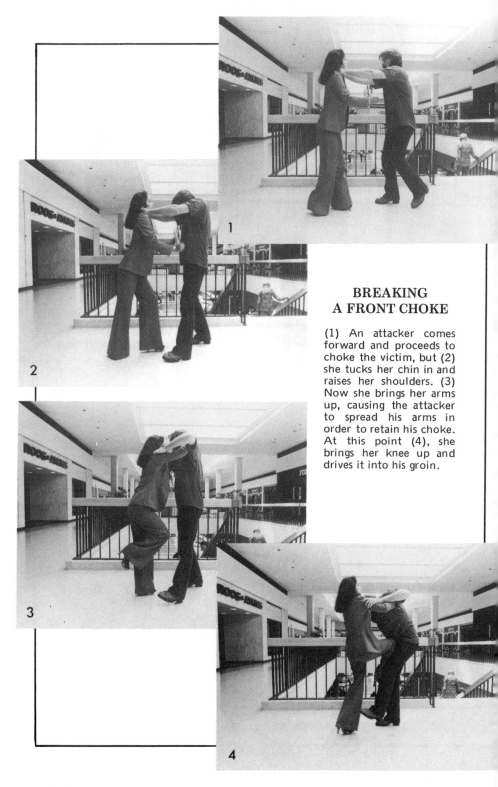

BREAKING A FRONT CHOKE

(1) An attacker comes forward and proceeds to choke the victim, but (2) she tucks her chin in and raises her shoulders. (3) Now she brings her arms up, causing the attacker to spread his arms in order to retain his choke. At this point (4), she brings her knee up and drives it into his groin.

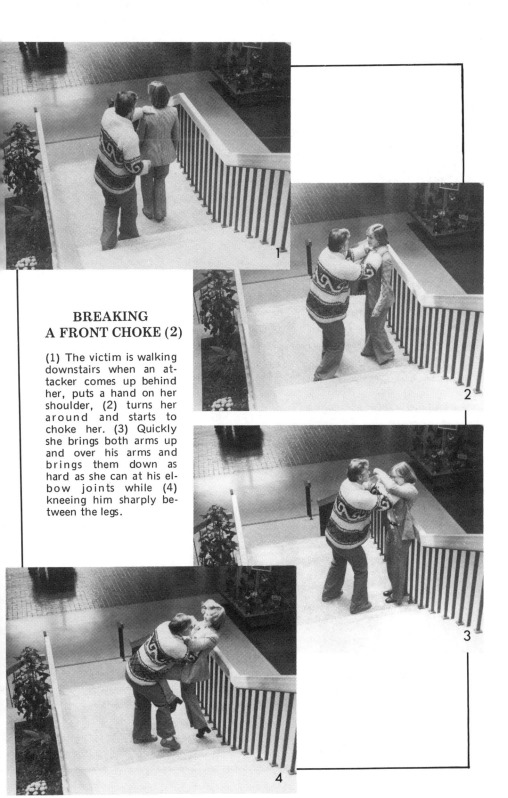

BREAKING
A FRONT CHOKE (2)

(1) The victim is walking downstairs when an attacker comes up behind her, puts a hand on her shoulder, (2) turns her around and starts to choke her. (3) Quickly she brings both arms up and over his arms and brings them down as hard as she can at his elbow joints while (4) kneeing him sharply between the legs.

1

2

WRIST GRAB ESCAPE

(1) The victim, walking through a shopping center, is grabbed at by a stranger who reaches out for her arm. (2) He snatches her wrist and pulls her into a doorway, but (3)

3

she steps around him and goes with the pull. While holding on to his grabbing arm, she brings her leg up, (4) following through with a knee to the groin.

4

GROCERY CART

(1) We see a housewife pushing a grocery cart down the aisle as a punk who is right in back of her (2) reaches in to grab her purse. (3) Quickly she turns the cart to-

wards the shelves, (4) hitting him with the cart and (5) knocking him off-balance. (6) She keeps pushing the cart and knocks him to the ground.

1

GROCERY BASKET

(1) Now we have a housewife using a basket to do her shopping. (2) As the attacker reaches in to grab her purse, (3) she grabs his hand and holds it while bringing her leg up, bending it at the knee, and kicks the attacker with a side kick.

2

3

BREAKING THE ATTACK TO ESCAPE

(1) We notice the victim walking in the shopping center when (2) suddenly she is confronted by an attacker who appears out of nowhere, grabs her around the waist and pulls her towards him. (3) She brings her forearm up sharply, striking him under the chin while lifting her leg and kneeing him hard in the groin.

CHAPTER IV

PERSONAL AND HOUSEHOLD ARTICLES AS WEAPONS

The contents of a woman's purse comprise a formidable arsenal. A pen, keys, glasses or a purse itself have all been used as effective weapons. Around the house, a book, magazine, newspaper or can of spray may be likewise effective. Almost any of these articles can be used to effect a quick stab or to deliver a telling strike. For example, provided you employ it quickly and accurately, the contents of a can of spray may be used to temporarily blind an assailant, giving you a chance to escape.

Let us say a stranger approaches and demands your purse. You might throw it hard, right in his face. Alternatively, as he reaches forward to grab your purse, you could kick him in the shin or groin. Taking still another approach, hold on to your purse, as he tugs against it. From such a position you can make use of this leverage by delivering a strong kick.

A rolled-up newspaper or magazine can be used as a club to keep the distance between you and your assailant. Distance is to your advantage in that it increases your chances for escaping, summoning help or assuming a more effective defensive position.

Like the martial arts weapon, the bo, a common household broom can be used very effectively for many different kinds of offensive and defensive situations. The rounded tip of the broom is particularly suitable for jabbing blows.

Your high-heeled shoes are useful in your hands to crack an attacker across the face, temples, throat, hands or groin. Above all, in an attack situation, do not hesitate to use any weapon as fiercely as possible. Use whatever comes to hand with all the speed and power available.

USING KEYS AS WEAPONS

(1) We note the young girl getting ready to get into her car when she is approached from the side. (2) When an attacker reaches for the door, she quickly strikes him in the eye with her keys, (3) causing him to turn away,

USING KEYS AS WEAPONS (2)

(1) Here we have a girl walking through the parking lot towards her car when she is approached by an attacker (2) who puts an arm around her shoulder.

holding his hand to his eye .   Note: In the close-up of the position of the keys (4), we see that all of the keys are inside her hand except for the one she strikes with.

(3) Quickly she turns around and, with keys in her hand, (4) strikes the attacker in the face.

SCHOOLBOOK ACROSS THE EYES

(1) We find the victim being approached from the rear while walking downstairs on her way to class. (2) The attacker attempts to grab her arm, but (3) she bends her elbow, then brings her leg up, bending it at the knee. (4) From

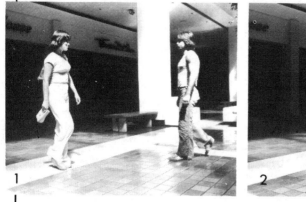

BOOK IN THE MOUTH

(1) A young girl walking through the shopping center with a paperback book in her hand notices a stranger staring at her purse. (2) When he reaches out to

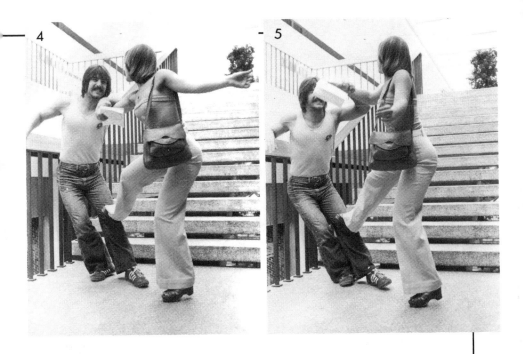

this position, she applies a side kick to his knee. Kicking first with power and speed, (5) she will follow up by striking her attacker across the eyes with her book.

grab it, she hangs the purse in the crook of her arm and (3) turns to face him, (4) striking the attacker across the mouth with the book.

SCHOOLBOOK
FOR DEFENSE

(1) A girl walking to class is approached by a stranger who (2) reaches out to grab her; she blocks his arm with her schoolbook and (3)

quickly uses both hands
to strike the attacker
across the bridge of his
nose, (4) knocking him
away from her.

1

NEWSPAPER DEFENSE

(1) Confronted by a stranger, the victim is holding a rolled-up newspaper. (2) When he steps forward to punch her, she blocks the blow with her left arm. (3) Continuing to restrain the attacker's punching arm, she draws her right arm back and, (4) bending slightly, sends a circular arching blow (5) to the attacker's groin. (6) As he doubles up, she brings her knee up, and (7) pushing on the back of his head, knees him in the face.

3

6

2

4

5

7

1

2

NEWSPAPER DEFENSE

(1) Now we see a young lady walking to her office with a rolled-up newspaper when she is confronted by a stranger who (2) reaches out and grabs her shoulder. (3) Tightening her grip on

3

the paper and blocking the attacker's arm, she (4) strikes him in the throat with the end of the newspaper, (5) knocking him to the floor.

4

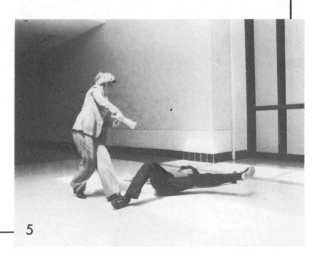

5

BROOM
FOR DEFENSE

(1) Here we have a store-owner sweeping the shop when she is approached by a stranger (2) who grabs her from the rear and attempts to turn her around. (3) She turns, but strikes him in the stomach with the tip of

the broom, causing him to bend forward. Then (4), quickly, she forces the broom upward, striking the attacker in the throat and (5) brings the bottom half of the broom up, striking him across the face.

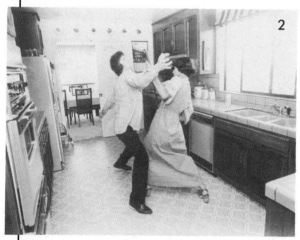

ATTACK
IN THE HOME

(1) We find an intruder walking into the kitchen while a woman is sweeping the floor. She doesn't show fear but takes a good grip on the broom. As he reaches out to grab her, (2) she moves forward, blocking his punch with the top part of the broom. Quickly she

brings the broom across, (3) striking him in the face with the top of the broom. (4) Now she forces him away with pressure from the broom and (5) directs the bottom half of the broom towards the attacker, (6) striking him in the groin.

PURSE AS A WEAPON

(1) Purse in hand, the senior citizen is going shopping when she is approached from the side by a stranger who asks for her purse, but she holds to it with both

3

hands until (2) he gets aggressive. She throws the purse in his face and (3) brings her right leg up, (4) kicking the attacker in the groin.

4

CONCLUSION

This book was written for the individual who doesn't have the time to enroll in a martial arts school. To become proficient in any of the martial arts would require not only that you find a good instructor but that you study and train for years.

In martial arts schools it is required that everyone work out with others of different sizes and different ability levels; yet this, because it provides the student the opportunity of working constantly with so many others, is the best way to learn how to handle yourself.

But if you are interested in learning as much as possible without the help of a professional instructor, you need a partner to assist you and help you go through the step-by-step movements in this book.

Some of the people who worked with me on this project had only one hour of instruction before we took the photographs. I used 27 people in the photo sessions, and of these only nine had previously had self-defense training.

So it is possible to learn out of this book if you can work out with someone else. You should regularly go through all the kicks and strikes in front of a mirror to check your speed, balance and posture. These are very important.

Basically, there are only three things that will be helpful in becoming proficient at self-defense. Practice. Practice. Practice.

WILLY CAHILL

7th-Degree Black Belt in Judo
10th-Degree Black Belt in Jujitsu
Black Belt Hall of Fame Judo Instructor of the Year
Jujitsu America Hall of Fame, Instructor of the Year
Judo coach, Cahill's Judo Academy
Judo coach, San Francisco State University
Judo coach, Stanford University
US coach, Junior Pan American Championships, 1976
US coach, World Championships, 1981, 1985, 1987, 1989, 1991
US coach, Pan American Games, 1983, 1987
US coach, Pacific Rim Championships, 1983, 1985
US Olympic Games Asst. coach, 1984, 1988
US coach, Goodwill Games, 1986, 1990
Member National Coaching Staff, US Judo Inc.
Director of Development, US Judo Inc.
Co-Founder of Jujitsu America